FINDING a CAREER

Careers If You Like History

Jenny MacKay

ReferencePoint Press®

San Diego, CA

About the Author
Jenny MacKay has written more than thirty books for teens and preteens on topics ranging from crime scene investigation and technological marvels to historical issues and the science of sports. She lives in Sparks, Nevada, with her husband, son, and daughter.

Picture Credits
Cover: Depositphotos
18: Thinkstock Images
31: Depositphotos
41: Depositphotos
67: Thinkstock Images

© 2017 ReferencePoint Press, Inc.
Printed in the United States

For more information, contact:
ReferencePoint Press, Inc.
PO Box 27779
San Diego, CA 92198
www.ReferencePointPress.com

LIBRARY OF CONGRESS CATALOGING-IN-PUBLICATION DATA

Name: MacKay, Jenny, 1978- author.
Title: Careers if you like history / by Jenny MacKay.
Description: San Diego, CA : ReferencePoint Press, Inc., 2017. | Series: Finding a career series | Includes bibliographical references and index.
Identifiers: LCCN 2015042817 (print) | LCCN 2015043381 (ebook) | ISBN 9781682820025 (hardback) | ISBN 9781682820032 (epub)
Subjects: LCSH: History--Vocational guidance.
Classification: LCC D16.19 .M35 2017 (print) | LCC D16.19 (ebook) | DDC 331.702--dc23

LC record available at http://lccn.loc.gov/2015042817

CONTENTS

Introduction: Futures for People Who Prefer to Learn About the Past

Students are increasingly nudged toward the so-called STEM careers—those that focus on science, technology, engineering, and math. The modern world hungers for new computer programs and apps, technological marvels, medical miracles, and scientific proof of everything in the universe. Requirements to graduate from high school or be accepted into colleges, universities, or vocational schools reflect the push for STEM. Students are expected to obtain a certain number of credits in the math and science classes that will carry them (and presumably the rest of human society) into the future in new and boundary-breaking ways.

But what if your interests are buried somewhere in the past? You might vastly prefer world history to geometry or physics. Architecture? Sure, you're interested in it, as long as it relates to the crumbling Colosseum of ancient Rome. Or maybe you're a Civil War buff, or you've read every book you can find about gangsters and the Mob during the Roaring Twenties, or your idea of the perfect vacation would be a week in Peru touring the ancient Incan ruins of Machu Picchu.

It's not that history classes are gone from the curriculum, but in today's STEM-focused and forward-facing world, history careers—and the people who work in them—are often painted as dusty, outdated, and on their way to extinction. As you study hard in your required STEM courses (as of course you should), your peers, parents, and other well-meaning people might raise their eyebrows if you proclaim that your true interests lie in bygone eras. You are bound to encounter questions about what you could possibly intend to do with your life if you study history. It can be fun to *read* about the past, people might tell you, but there's no *future* in it.

Critical Thinkers and Problem Solvers

Rest assured, though, that people with a passion for history land in a wide variety of fascinating careers. The type of people who are interested in history ask thoughtful questions and consider various ways to answer them. They are good at seeing things from many different perspectives, imagining themselves in other people's shoes, and explaining their reasoning in logical and compelling ways. They prefer asking questions that start with "why" and "how," and this helps them open up the past to make it relevant to the present or even the future. History buffs also tend to be good at recognizing patterns. They are the kind of people who draw surprising connections between seemingly unrelated details. In addition, they develop excellent writing and speaking abilities, since they take pride in presenting their insights and discoveries both on paper and in person.

People with a knack for studying history often excel at connecting ideas, finding and prioritizing solutions to difficult issues, and spying errors in other people's reasoning. In short, they tend to be good at solving problems, which is a talent employers covet. "Our best employees are problem solvers and are able to weave everything they know together," Marie Artim, vice president of talent acquisition at Enterprise Rent-A-Car, said in a January 2015 *Washington Post* article. As of 2015 Enterprise had hired more entry-level college graduates each year than any other US company. "They can think on their feet," Artim adds.

Combine that with the ability to express ideas well in writing and in speech, and people who study history impress potential employers in many different fields. You might find history fanatics working for foreign embassies and government intelligence agencies, on the sets of movies and presidential press conferences, on the site of an archaeological dig in Egypt, and behind the scenes of the *Apollo 11* spaceship exhibit at the Smithsonian National Air and Space Museum in Washington, DC. Historians find careers in obvious places like museums and libraries but also in politics, the military, medicine, arts, science, business, law, and construction.

Seeing the Big Picture

In a rapidly modernizing world where human beings are connected globally like never before, it's not enough to invent technology that spans oceans and continents. Employers want people who can pull the pieces together, see the big picture, and remember where humanity came from in order to decide where it should go. Brendan Troy, who graduated from Vanderbilt University with a history degree in 1996, says his ability to think is fundamental to his career as an investment banker. "Do I still draw on the plight of the Russian peasant in the late 19th century in my daily experience on Wall Street?" he says on the university's history department website. "The answer is obviously no, but I do remember that Professor Wcislo made me think more about root causes."

The ability to analyze why things have happened leads to predicting what might come next. This is where history buffs really shine. So when someone asks what you could possibly plan to do with a background in history, you can retort that it's obvious—you plan to help shape a better tomorrow.

Federal Historian

Why Does the Government Need Historians?

The government creates a massive amount of information—in the form of reports, statistics, fact sheets, laws, and more. All federal laws, for example, are compiled in a massive collection called the *Statutes at Large*. The justice system keeps careful records of all decisions by judges and all verdicts by juries. Federal museums store historical documents and catalog other items of historical interest. They also compose text for exhibits and websites so visitors can learn about the history of the nation and its place in the world. Being a free society, the American public likes to have access to these historical records so people can educate themselves and others. Government officials, too, need to examine historical data for analysis, discussion, and decision making on issues large and small. To these ends, the federal government employs people who gather up and sift through massive amounts of historical resources to find, summarize, and share important information. These individuals are federal historians.

All Government Branches Have Historians

Not every federal historian does the same thing, but most will be involved in the researching and writing up of histories. All three government branches—lawmakers, the justice system, and the executive branch—employ historians. Congress, the lawmaking body of the United States, has two departments focused on history: the US Senate Historical Office and the US House of Representatives History, Art & Archives. Historians in these departments collect and maintain biographical information about every senator and representative who has ever served. They also record details of important laws, events, and eras that have shaped national history.

Historians also work for the executive branch, which encompasses the president, vice president, and cabinet posts such as the secretary of the treasury and the secretary of state. These distinct offices may call upon historians to find and write up details about past events that seem to bear on current executive matters. Perhaps the most obvious function for a historian serving the executive branch is to provide facts and other historical material for presidential speeches. However, other work is equally important. For example, if the US Department of State wished to review the opening of trade relations with China during the 1960s and 1970s in order to rethink or retune current trade strategies, it would call upon the Office of the Historian to pull records from its multivolume *Foreign Relations of the United States*. From this work, it could review memoranda from key players such as President Richard Nixon or Henry Kissinger (who was assistant for national security affairs at the time and later became secretary of state) to see how the executive office brokered better relations with the Chinese.

Historians are equally important to the judicial branch, which includes the US Supreme Court—the place where the nation's most significant legal battles are waged. Historians working for this branch compile and maintain biographical information about every Supreme Court justice and attorney general. They also chronicle all legal cases that make it to the highest court in the land. One of their most important roles is fulfilling research requests by justices, attorneys, the press, and the general public about past legal cases that could affect current ones.

Defense and Intelligence Specialists

If you are more interested in national security than legal or legislative battles, both the military and the Secret Service utilize historians. Each branch of the armed forces has its own department dedicated to history and employs researchers to compile and maintain detailed military records. The army compiles and publishes its *Annual Historical Report* that adds details to the lengthy history of each specific unit in the service. The army's Historical Resources Branch also serves the Army Staff with specific recorded details about deployed units. Historians who work with such records may locate information that can assist military leaders as they formulate strategies to deal with current conflicts and problems.

If you are more interested in covert operations, the CIA employs history specialists, too. However, it may take several years

Recording the Facts but Staying Neutral

"When a federal historian is writing a scholarly article as an authority in the field, he or she enjoys the same degree of editorial freedom as do scholars in academia. . . . [However,] federal historians, whether civil servants or contractors, do not speak or write from a personal viewpoint when acting in their official capacities on matters that have political consequence for their agencies. Their work, whether an exhibit, a book, an article, or a web site, is subject to review and approval by agency administrators."

Victoria A. Harden, "What Do Federal Historians Do?," *Perspectives on History*, May 1999. www.historians.org.

to obtain government clearance to handle secret records. Some historians who work with the CIA are former military or intelligence officers, which helps speed clearance along. Even the history records themselves often need clearance before they are made available to the public. CIA histories of US involvement in Indochina during the 1950s, 1960s, and 1970s weren't declassified until 2009, for example. Beyond writing histories of CIA activities, historians in this agency might instead work at the CIA Museum in Washington, DC. Here, they collect and display clothing, weapons, and other artifacts related to the agency and its missions.

The Work of a Federal Historian

Much of a government historian's job involves fulfilling tasks assigned by government officials. A senator who wants to propose legislation regarding the use of federal land may ask a congressional historian to compose a research paper on the history of that land and its former uses. The president's press secretary, a high-ranking military officer, or any number of other people might request a historical summary of a particular issue. Federal historians must have a broad knowledge of history and find information quickly. This is as true today as it was in May 1999, when Victoria A. Harden, a former director of the Office of NIH History and the Stetten Museum at the National Institutes of Health, wrote in a *Perspectives on History* editorial, "Federal historians are expected to be generalists with respect to the agencies with which they work and must be able to answer questions from three years ago as easily as from a hundred years ago." They must know their way around archives of historical information and be able to pick out what they need, often on a tight deadline, in order to write up summaries or briefs of historical facts and details for the officials who requested them.

The work of some federal historians is used by specialists within their agencies, and therefore it doesn't get seen by the public. Even if the information is not classified, few members of the public would seek out such information. That does not mean, however, that all federal historians produce information that remains largely unseen outside government agencies. Sometimes federal historians might be tasked with curating an event or providing information for public brochures. The White House, for example, has a curatorial staff of historians who draft information for the president as well as for the tour guides who share information with tour groups passing through this famous residence. Similarly, federal historians are not always hidden away in dusty government archives. At any time, historians could be asked to present information to groups of officials or other dignitaries. They might teach a seminar to a group of staff members or lawmakers on a particular subject, or they could be called into a highly classified meeting to present the results of their research on a topic. To that end, they should be as comfortable speaking in front of groups as poring over historical records.

Whether their efforts are used to help shape public policy or to fill White House tour pamphlets, the role of federal historians is usually to inform, not advise. They find and summarize the facts but leave interpretation up to others, especially if the consequences of their findings are being used by agencies to advocate a political position. This separates them from general history writers or university history professors, who typically argue for a specific view of a historical event.

Education and Skills You'll Need for Getting a Job

If you want a job as a federal historian, you should plan to pursue an advanced degree in history. A master's degree is typical for entry-level positions such as lower-level curators, librarians, and records managers; a PhD may be necessary for roles with greater responsibility. Preferably, you should specialize in an area of history closely related to the governmental branch or department you want to work for. Military historians, for example, might be interested in working for the National Park Service, with its oversight of historical battlefields. Legal historians would

How the Work of a Federal Historian Is Used

"When the [state department's *Foreign Relations of the United States*] series first started, it was primarily an internal audience within the state department as working documents. As the series evolved, I would say that at this point there are several primary audiences. First of all, you have policymakers . . . across the government, studying the antecedents to the issues that they are now working on. . . . The educational establishment: When I was at the National Defense University, for example, we used the material . . . to teach the upcoming senior leadership of the government and the military about strategic decision-making and how the government works. [But] the most visible and active, I think, audience is the academic community."

CSPAN , interview with Stephen Randolph, C-SPAN, October 21, 2013. www.c-span.org.

perhaps be most attracted to the offices of the judicial branch of government. Because the various government agencies have diverse focuses, good candidates for historians in these offices may need more than a knowledge of history to obtain a job. Historians working with foreign affairs or aspects of foreign history might wish to have appropriate foreign language training. Likewise, expertise in economics or political science can benefit those looking to work in congressional offices that contend with these issues.

Probably the most important skill for federal historians is the ability to quickly (and accurately) research a topic, write up the findings, and present them to various audiences and in various formats. Strong writing and speaking skills are critical. The ability to prioritize is also important. Federal historians are usually juggling numerous projects at any given time, and certain deadlines (such as a request from the president's staff for a briefing on a particular subject) will take priority over others. As Harden explains:

Timetables for historical projects are dictated by agency needs . . . and are often exceedingly short. Federal historians, whether civil servants or contractors, are accustomed to conducting research and producing documents on extraordinarily tight deadlines—days or hours, in some cases. Knowing where to find materials quickly, and close attention to accuracy of the written document that results are the requisites for this aspect of federal history jobs.

Working on such deadlines can be stressful, so working well under pressure can be as important to success in this job as historical knowledge.

Finding a Job

Historians who work for the federal government will have what is known as a classified position—one assigned to a particular level of pay and responsibility. Entry-level historians typically attend to simpler research tasks and have fewer responsibilities and speaking requirements than do historians who are hired at or promoted to higher levels of classification.

Since federal historians work for the government on assigned tasks, they might work in conjunction with other nongovernmental historians to complete these tasks. These nongovernmental consultants are employed temporarily and are paid per assignment. They might be hired for a project because of their particular expertise, and for the duration of the project, these individuals take on the role and title of federal historian. However, these consultants are free to refuse projects, allowing them to pursue outside interests. Full-time governmental historians are not free to decline assigned tasks, although many are able to work on outside projects on their own time—unless such projects were to deal with classified information obtained through their function as a government employee.

Whether federal historians are employed by the government or work as independent consultants, they typically live in or near

Washington, DC, because they must be near the public records for their research and also the people to whom they must present their findings. A willingness to travel is important as well, since some research tasks or projects may require visiting places around the nation or even in other countries.

Do Federal Historians Make a Good Living?

Although many governmental agencies employ historians, there are a limited number of available positions, and the competition for them can be intense. Furthermore, employees who do get jobs working as historians for the government tend to stay on and work their way up to higher levels of responsibility.

Historians working as classified employees for the government earn a specific salary based on their level of classification. On average, federal historians working for the executive branch in the Washington, DC, area earn a yearly salary of about $90,000. Entry-level historians, of course, can expect to make less than that, and historians with more experience might earn higher salaries. In addition to receiving a standard, predictable, and reliable paycheck, historians employed by the government also receive benefits like health insurance, retirement plans, and guaranteed vacation time. Such pay and benefits are not afforded to consultants who hold the title of federal historian on a temporary basis.

Preserving and Sharing the Story of the Nation

Federal historians create an important link between the government and the governed. Some keep the public informed about what happens behind the doors of government offices. Others help members of the government stay informed so that they can argue for effective public policy. Still others directly teach or inform the public by presenting information used in museums, journals, or even books available to everyone. They preserve the story of the nation and share it with all who are interested in finding out more about America's unique heritage.

Find Out More

National Council on Public History (NCPH)
127 Cavanaugh Hall-IUPUI
425 University Blvd.
Indianapolis, IN 46202
phone: (317) 274-2716
website: http://ncph.org

The NCPH seeks to build a community of historians, provide them with professional skills and tools, improve the practice of preserving history, and advocate for history and historians.

Society for History in the Federal Government
Box 14139
Benjamin Franklin Station
Washington, DC 20044
website: http://shfg.org/shfg

Founded in 1979, the society is an active group of historians and also archaeologists, museum curators, editors, and many others who are committed to studying the history of the American government.

Supreme Court Historical Society
224 E. Capitol St. NE
Washington, DC 20003
phone: (202) 543-0400
website: www.supremecourthistory.org

Since 1974 this private, nonprofit organization has worked to collect and preserve all history related to the Supreme Court of the United States.

US House of Representatives History, Art & Archives
US Capitol, Room H154
Washington, DC 20515-6601
phone: (202) 225-7000
website: http://history.house.gov

The US House of Representatives' Office of the Historian and Office of Art and Archives work together to serve as the House's institutional memory. They provide important historical support and resources for members of Congress, their staff, and the general public.

US Senate Historical Office
201 Hart Senate Office Building
Washington, DC 20510-7108
phone: (202) 224-6900
website: www.senate.gov/artandhistory/history/common/
generic/Senate_Historical_Office.htm

The US Senate Historical Office collects and provides information about current and past activities that is used to advise senators and committees in their policy-making endeavors.

Teacher

A Few Facts

Number of Jobs
More than 125,000 social sciences teachers in public high schools and about 24,000 postsecondary history professors

Degrees
More than half of public high school social sciences teachers have a master's degree

Salaries
High school history teachers make an average salary of $56,000; college history professors make an average of $76,000

Hours
On average, teachers work about fifty-two hours per week

Future Job Outlook
For high school history teachers, about 6 percent growth rate through 2024, which is roughly average growth when compared to other professions

Not All History Instructors Are Alike

Here's a common scenario: You're talking about your love of history and you let it slip that you might even major in history in college. The next thing you hear is: *Other than teaching, what can you do with a history degree?* But teaching history can be fun, fascinating, and energizing. People who have a passion for history often find that inspiring others to learn about the past—and therefore better understand the present—is more rewarding than they could ever have imagined.

Not all history educators have identical jobs, of course. In middle schools and high schools, social studies teachers instruct students about local, state, national, and global history as well as civics and geography. The scope of the material is broad, and effective teachers must figure out the best way to leave their students with more than a mere memorization of names and dates. Social studies teachers show how historical events are connected, how the struggles of the past may still be a part of today's controversies, and how historical events or civic policies

Students listen intently to a class lecture. Those who teach history and social studies must be able to clearly explain events, ideas, and principles to students who may or may not share a passion for history.

have been shaped by the actions of concerned individuals. "There is probably no more important skill required in teaching social studies than the ability to explain events, ideas, principles, and social interrelationships," says Florida social studies teacher Bob Kizlik on his own ADPRIMA webpage. "Helping students make new connections, to find challenge and meaning in social studies content is what excellent social studies teachers do every day."

Most social studies teachers understand that students will resist learning about the past, arguing that it is no longer relevant. However, good history educators seek to show students how the past is a vital force by connecting it to the issues of today. In an April 24, 2012, *Education Week* interview, Bill Bigelow, a curriculum editor for *Rethinking Schools* magazine, advises teachers to "teach about what matters. Our job is to excite students about the world, to help them see the role that they can play in making society more equal and more just, to express their ideas powerfully, to see that social studies is about real people's lives and about their relationship to each other and to nature." One year of high school history, for example, is usually devoted specifically to the US government to give students an understanding of how government works and of the advantages of participating in the operation of government, whether through voting or by running for office.

Many of these skills are also practiced by college and university history professors. In these institutions, though, professors tend to focus on specific areas of history that they have mastered. These areas might range from medieval European history to the history of popular culture in modern Japan. Most college or university students are required to take certain general history courses, but others might choose to specialize in classes with a narrower focus. Yale University, for example, offers more than two hundred different history courses every semester, including Significance of American Slavery, American Environmental History, and Making of the Modern Middle East.

The sheer range of topics—from art history to the history of medicine—means that if you wish to teach history, you should know what fields interest you. You will also have to decide whether you want to explain what you have learned in a secondary school classroom or a college-level seminar. That is, you must decide where you think you can make the biggest impact on the next generation of history enthusiasts as well as active and informed participants in a modern democracy.

What Makes a Good History Teacher?

At any level of education, history teachers need certain special skills and personality traits to succeed at their job. They must be experts in the subjects they teach. They should be skilled at research and also writing, since they must teach their students how to do both things. Most important, good history teachers have a knack for public speaking and for making history interesting. Even the world's foremost expert on the history of ancient Egypt will not be a good teacher if his or her lessons about pyramids are painfully dull. If you set your sights on a teaching career, an energetic personality will be a strong ally. A sense of humor is valuable, too

Teaching a Love of History

"The number-one thing is, you have to know history to actually teach it. That seems like an obvious point, but sometimes it's ignored in schools. Even more than that, I think it's important that people who are teaching history do have training in history. A lot of times people have education degrees, which have not actually provided them with a lot of training in the subject. They know a lot about methodology. [That's] important, but . . . the key thing is really to love the subject, to be able to convey that to your students, and if you can do that, I think you'll be a great teacher."

Eric Foner, quoted in David Cutler, "You Have to Know History to Actually Teach It," *Atlantic*, January 10, 2014. www.theatlantic.com.

(for any teachers—not just history teachers), as is the ability to recall facts quickly and think creatively on the spot.

History teachers must also be comfortable with speaking to groups. That is why a history teacher is not always the same as a history buff. Communicating ideas is key. Like all teachers, history teachers must be able to connect with students and share ideas that matter. In the April 2012 *Education Week* interview, Stephen Lazar, a social studies teacher in Brooklyn, says that a good way for history teachers to prepare for their lessons is to ask, "'What do I want my students to remember about this unit in ten years?' and 'How can my students use the information and skills outside of my class right now?'" Helping students recognize such goals requires good speaking skills. It is equally important to be an attentive listener because students will have questions and concerns of their own that you must be able not only to answer but to connect back to the topic of discussion.

Education and Credentials

Landing a good job in front of your own classroom requires spending time in other people's classrooms first. Teaching history in a public middle school or high school requires a teaching credential in a single subject (in contrast, elementary schools require a multiple-subject credential). Every state issues its own teaching credentials, and their requirements may slightly differ, but generally, a credential requires a bachelor's degree in education with a certain number of courses in history (or a degree in history with additional classes in education). Prospective teachers then must complete an internship, often called student teaching, which usually lasts half of a school year. States may have other requirements such as criminal background checks and passing subject-matter tests in history before they issue a credential or certification allowing a person to teach in that state. Teachers certified in one state can usually obtain a teaching credential in another state fairly easily if they move during their career.

If you want to teach history at a college or university, you should plan to earn at least a master's degree in the subject, which is the minimum qualification to teach at the college level. Most universities require their faculty members to have a doctorate in history with a specialization in a particular topic, era, or geographic location. Acquiring a position and advancing through the various ranks of professorship often require prospective candidates to prove their contribution to the field through published works or other scholarly activities.

The Work of History Teachers

Most teachers, no matter what level they teach, are in class Monday through Friday. At the secondary level, teaching is a daytime job. At the college level, it can also include nights. And, yes, teachers get lots of school holidays and summers off. But hours spent with students in the classroom are only part of the teacher's day. Many teachers and professors spend extra hours every day preparing lessons and activities for their students.

At the university level, in addition to teaching, history professors often conduct research projects. As experts in their field, they may also write articles or books for publication. They may do this work during summer breaks from school or during a sabbatical—a period when they do no teaching because they are instead working on a research or writing project, especially one that requires travel. It is important to realize that teachers usually have many more duties and responsibilities than what their students see.

Increasingly, many teachers, especially at the college level, have become involved in online teaching, which changes the nature of their workday. Rather than physically going to classrooms, these instructors may create online courses for their students, a task that requires them to have excellent writing skills and be very familiar with technology. Online teaching gives history instructors a lot of flexibility in their work schedules and even lets them live far away from their students or travel for research while still being able to teach courses.

Making a Modern Living Teaching About the Past

Teaching is often considered one of the lower-paying professions that require a college degree, but it is definitely possible to earn a living by teaching. The average income nationally for middle and high school teachers is $55,000 a year. Although most states have a pay scale for teachers, and brand-new ones earn a starting salary less than this average (usually about $35,000 a year), the longer you teach, the more you typically earn. Teachers in grades K–12 who complete an advanced degree (a master's degree or a doctorate) also earn a higher salary in most states. States typically also provide their full-time K–12 teachers with good benefits, including health insurance and a retirement plan.

Income for instructors at the college or university level can have a wider range. Many history professors are employed part-time as adjunct faculty and teach in addition to another job, or they might teach for multiple schools. Other history professors are given tenure at their institution, which means they are full-time, permanent employees who earn a steady salary and typically receive a package of benefits like health insurance and retirement plans. On average, tenured professors can expect to earn about $75,000 or more. However, most colleges and universities offer only a limited number of full-time, tenured positions, usually only to instructors who have taught at the institution for many years and who have a doctorate.

Some history teachers or professors earn extra income by writing books or articles for magazines, journals, and other publications. Those with advanced degrees who are considered experts in a particular history topic might also get paid to be consultants for the government (local, state, or federal) as well as for museums and other institutions, or they can be hired to give speeches and presentations at conferences and other events. In addition, many history educators, particularly at the college level, apply for and receive research grants—money paid by the government, a private foundation, a nonprofit organization, or another source—to pay for the expenses of a research project they wish to conduct. Grants are not usually considered income, but they can make it affordable for history instructors to travel and do research on topics that interest them.

Choose Your College History Specialization Wisely

"At the [undergraduate] level, students do not usually declare a specialty, though most history majors have some idea of fields that interest them by the time they finish their undergraduate education. . . . At the doctoral level there is much greater specialization, and PhD students typically declare a major field, a minor field, and an area of special concentration. I strongly encourage people entering the field to choose at least one of these specializations in a field that is expanding. Unfortunately the world has far too many US and European historians, and students who gain experience in fields such as Latin American, African, Middle Eastern, or Asian histories have greater opportunities when they hit the job market."

Michael E. Brooks, "Advice on How to Become a History Professor," *historymike* (blog), December 5, 2009. http://historymike.blogspot.com.

Are History Teachers in Demand?

Because history is a subject all students generally have to take in middle school, high school, and during their undergraduate years in college, there is a steady need for history teachers. It is usually possible for history teachers to find a job, although it helps if they are willing to teach at any school or at any grade level for which they are qualified. Having the ability to teach another related subject such as English, a foreign language, or government can increase the chances of finding a teaching job.

If you wish to teach history at the university level, you must be willing to go where openings occur. Competition for professorships is high, and there are always many prospective candidates for the few open positions. In addition, universities often seek candidates in a particular field of study that their history department lacks. For example, a university might have an opening for scholars of medieval history or North African history but not twentieth-century American history. Therefore, your specialization can limit the jobs for which you are qualified to apply. However, with patience and tenacity, teachers do get jobs that prove to be rewarding, giving them a chance to expand their own academic interests while passing on their knowledge and love of history to their students.

Find Out More

American Association of University Professors (AAUP)
1133 Nineteenth St. NW, Suite 200
Washington, DC 20036
phone: (202) 737-5900
website: www.aaup.org

The AAUP is an organization of university and college professors in all academic disciplines, including history. It stands up for the rights and values of all those who teach or do research for institutions of higher education.

National Council for History Education (NCHE)

13940 Cedar Rd. #393
University Heights, OH 44118
phone: (240) 696-6600
website: www.nche.net

The main goal of the NCHE is to bring together history teachers, community leaders, museums, archives, libraries, and historical societies to ensure excellence in history education for all ages.

National History Education Clearinghouse

Roy Rosenzweig Center for History and New Media
4400 University Dr., MSN 1E7
Fairfax, VA 22030
phone: (703) 993-9277
website: http://teachinghistory.org

A project of the Roy Rosenzweig Center for History and New Media at George Mason University, the National History Education Clearinghouse provides resources to help K–12 history teachers improve techniques for teaching US history.

Organization of History Teachers

1690 Newtown-Langhorne Rd.
Newtown, PA 18940-2414
phone: (215) 968-3913
website: www.historians.org/about-aha-and-membership/
affiliated-societies/organization-of-history-teachers

This organization helps history teachers from kindergarten through twelfth grade find professional opportunities. It also advocates for history in the K–12 curriculum.

Society for History Education (SHE)

Department of History
CSULB—1250 Bellflower Blvd.
Long Beach, CA 90840-1601
phone: (562) 985-4428
website: www.societyforhistoryeducation.org

SHE provides support to history teachers in America and abroad and publishes *The History Teacher*, a quarterly journal providing inspiration and techniques for history education.

Librarian and Archivist

Inside Libraries and Archives

Since human beings first learned to draw and write, they have created documents and images to record their experiences. Books, manuscripts, paintings, photographs, maps, and other records tell the story of civilization. Nations have sought to store these items to preserve their historical importance. Archivists and librarians carry out the task of maintaining the collection of such records, helping ensure that they are available for public inspection while at the same time passed on to future generations.

Libraries and archives house published materials—mainly books, newspapers, and magazines but also audiovisual material like films, documentaries, and recordings of speeches. Libraries help circulate copies of these items to anyone who wishes to examine them. Public libraries, for example, lend books, films, or audio recordings to patrons from the local community. School libraries hold collections of works of interest to students. Colleges and universities hold large and extensive libraries with materials their students can use for research papers and projects.

Some organizations and private institutions keep libraries of works available to their members that are related to their goals and fields of interest.

Archives are a different kind of place where documents and resources are stored. They differ from libraries because they hold original copies of historical records, such as diaries and journals, photographs, pamphlets, sketches, drawings, and even film footage of a significant event. Most resources in a library can be replaced if they are damaged or worn out, but the materials in an archive cannot. Therefore, archives typically do not lend their holdings to the public; someone interested in seeing items in an archive usually must travel to the archive and schedule an appointment. Occasionally, archives do lend parts of their collections to museums for temporary exhibit. The National Archives in Washington, DC, holds the Declaration of Independence, for example, while the UCLA Film & Television Archive stores three hundred thousand film prints and also works to restore older prints to keep them from decaying. Archivists and librarians both help the public access information, but they work in different ways, and their jobs require different tasks.

What Do Librarians and Archivists Do?

Librarians have a great many duties that go far beyond sorting and shelving books. Increasingly, they are technology specialists who show library visitors how to use the Internet, navigate social media sites, or even file their taxes online. Librarians serve as teachers, frequently reading to small children or presenting free workshops to adults on all sorts of topics. They also organize entertaining programs, concerts, and other events for people of all ages.

Librarians are businesspeople, too. They make decisions about the best new books, magazine subscriptions, resources, and technology to buy while staying within the library's budget. They read widely and ensure that the books and other materials the library offers are up-to-date and relevant. They constantly review what the library offers and seek new ways to provide information

Archivists Collect and Preserve History

"There's sometimes a conception that we just take in a few books here and there—it can be anything from a single carrier bag left on the doorstep to a few van loads of records. During some recent maintenance work we had to empty one storage unit—this came to just over 600 volumes! The work can be heavy and really dirty as well. . . . It's an amazing feeling, being responsible for nearly 1,000 years of history. It's daunting—but thrilling—to think that everything we keep, we keep forever."

Gary Brannan, "A Day in the Life of an Archivist," National Archives, November 20, 2013. http://blog.nationalarchives.gov.uk.

to visitors. They must be good marketers and networkers as well, actively promoting their library.

Archivists are much less visible within their communities because most of the public does not routinely visit an archive. Archives can be big or small, and depending on the size of the holdings, they may be housed in stand-alone structures or in a room in a building used for multiple purposes. Cities may have an archive of their historical documents that is located somewhere in a government office building. The National Archives is an agency of the federal government and has its own buildings where records are kept. Some institutions and universities might have rooms or floors devoted to their own archived collections. Many of these archives can be accessed by the public, but usually only those doing research on a specific topic seek out these collections.

Archivists make decisions about what resources to collect and keep in the archives, for example, although they may base their decisions on historical importance rather than their visitors' preferences. Like librarians, archivists carefully organize and store materials so they are easy to find. Also like librarians, archivists help visitors find resources, whether those are lyrics a famous songwriter jotted down on a cocktail napkin or the original business ledgers of a shop with a two-hundred-year history.

Archivists often work with materials that are old and some-times fragile. They preserve and protect these materials by put-ting them in containers or other storage devices that prevent or delay deterioration. Some of the most delicate of these can only be seen and not touched, or if visitors are permitted to handle the items, they might have to do so under careful supervision. Some archives, though, are chiefly digital, which allows the public to inspect these items—whether originals or copies of nondigital works—without concern for theft or damage.

Both librarians and archivists must be familiar with the digital storing and retrieving of information. Because many publications and records have moved from print to digital format, librarians have to be trained in accessing these resources and pointing pa-trons to them. In a 2011 interview on the Practising Law Institute blog site, Karen Carter, a graduate in library and information sci-ence, notes, "Anyone can get just about anything at their finger-tips now, so librarians have to adjust to having changed roles in the lives of users, perhaps changing from the go-to person for information to being a teacher/guide to help people both navi-gate information sources and use current tools to maximize their information-seeking." Some patrons may even prefer to visit a library or archive web page rather than a physical building, so librarians and archivists should be accustomed to helping people online as well.

A Typical Workday in an Archive

Archivists have many duties to protect and grow their collections, but they also help the public access these collections. A typical day for an archivist might include acquiring new works for a col-lection, figuring out how to preserve the items already within the collection, and overseeing an exhibit of materials from it. In a 2012 interview with the Moving Image Archive News website, Giovanna Fossati, an archivist for the EYE Film Institute in the Netherlands, explains the scope of her duties: "I am responsible for developing and monitoring policies with regards to the collection and I have the curatorial responsibility of the activities related to acquisition, selection, preservation, restoration, and on-line access and presentation. I am also in charge of academic and R&D [research and development] projects and contacts with international academic networks." Since Fossati deals with film, she works with getting rare films exhibited—sometimes over the Internet, sometimes in curated installations—so that more of the public has a chance to see them. Document archivists, on the other hand, may deal with a few scholars who wish to see a specific letter written by a famous author, and thus exhibition may not be their aim. Still, digitalization is making it possible for document and image archivists to permit greater public access to their holdings.

Archivists, especially of small institutions, may work alone or with a few other people. Most of their work is done within the archive itself. However, archivists may be called out of the office to examine potential documents or records they might want to add to their collections.

A Typical Workday in a Library

Librarians might start the day reading book catalogs and reviewing new material the library might want to buy. Librarians must know their patrons well in order to make purchases that meet the needs of their communities. School and university librarians, for example, have to know what students are studying to make sure the library has appropriate resources.

Much of the typical day will be spent assisting patrons with finding materials. This might include helping locate books on a library shelf or helping find information on the Internet. Knowing history can help librarians make connections to find information that their patrons may not be aware of. Academic and community librarians also might spend part of their day organizing and supervising events held at the library. These might be reading events such as preschool story time or an afternoon book club for senior citizens.

Librarians might also serve as marketers, making their communities aware of library programs and other offerings. For instance,

A librarian works with a student on a class project. Librarians and archivists maintain collections of all sorts of published materials—both print and digital—and provide help with research projects, navigating online sources, and information gathering.

they might have to update a library web page or add comments to a library blog to announce an author visit or a display of local artwork within the library. They might even have to reach out to businesses and organizations within their communities to bring attention to what their library offers.

Training to Become an Archivist or Librarian

Librarians and archivists both require specialized education and training. An archivist typically needs at least a bachelor's degree, usually in a field such as art, history, library science, or archival science. Several universities and colleges (including online institutions) offer advanced degrees in archival science that train individuals in everything from archive theory to conservation to Internet technology. A master's degree in archival science or a related field will help aspiring archivists to find a job. A special certification, such as that of a digital archives specialist, can improve the chances of finding a job in this field. Completing an internship can also provide special training and connections that will be valuable when looking for employment.

People interested in becoming librarians should plan on ultimately completing a master's degree in library science following their bachelor's degree. It is usually helpful for the undergraduate degree to be in something *other* than library science—such as education, history, psychology, or language arts. This can make an applicant more attractive to potential employers. To work as a school librarian, particularly in a K–12 school, a bachelor's degree in education is desirable or may even be required.

In addition to a master's degree, certification as a librarian or media specialist may be an advantage when seeking a library job. In some states, all librarians are required to have such a certification. In other states, certifications may only be required for certain types of librarians, such as in schools.

What Is the Likelihood of Getting a Job?

Federal, state, and local governments, as well as museums, colleges, universities, religious institutions, historical societies, and businesses, all hire archivists, although institutions with small archives may only need one employee—or even a part-time one. Therefore, the need for archivists is steady, but there are not likely to be many open positions in this field. Someone seeking a job as an archivist may need to wait for a position to open because the current archivist has left or retired. Competition for a vacant archivist position can be intense.

Most towns, cities, counties, states, schools, colleges, and universities have libraries and employ librarians, so there are multiple places for aspiring librarians to apply for jobs. However, the traditional role of the librarian has changed. No longer is a librarian simply an individual whose chief responsibility is to check out books. Nowadays librarians are experts in information science, which encompasses the many ways in which information is distributed. As more people are able to access books and other printed resources online, fewer people need to visit libraries to

Librarians Wear Many Hats

"As (librarians), we help to teach people how to become self-sufficient on the computer, find the answer to patron's questions (no offense Google, but while you may come back with a million answers, we librarians come back with the right answer), develop graphic designs for advertisement, act as social media managers, handle reader's advisory, teach information literacy classes, act as storytellers, and teach children, to name just a few of our duties. We wear many, many caps."

Rebecca Tischler, "5 Things That People Don't Realize Their Librarians Do," INALJ, April 10, 2014. http://inalj.com.

find information. Libraries do still remain important resources in schools and communities, offering people a place to gather, study, learn, and access technology they might not have at home, but librarians must be educated in the digital realm so that they can meet the needs of patrons who may not ever set foot in a library building. Thus, if you are interested in becoming a librarian, you should learn as much about the digital offerings of libraries as the physical resources. Since competition for library jobs is strong, being well versed in information systems and the retrieval of all sorts of information resources will help you in landing a job.

Because the modern world—the information age—depends on access to information, librarians and archivists remain important to society. While library budgets have tightened and digital resources increased, many people have assumed libraries would disappear. However, most Americans still value libraries. A recent Pew Research Center poll found that 90 percent of Americans believed the closing of a public library would have a major impact on their communities, and 81 percent agreed that libraries provide services that people would have a hard time finding elsewhere. Perhaps it is better to see the changes within libraries as an evolution in the services provided. Libraries may have fewer magazines on shelves, but they have volumes upon volumes—stretching back decades—on digital resources. As a future librarian, you will be more familiar with this evolution because you have lived in an age when such changes seem commonplace. Likewise, the fact that entire archives of works and images are available digitally is not surprising to anyone who has grown up in an age dominated by the Internet. As a new librarian or archivist, it will be your job to help organize these resources and help people locate them in a culture in which the amount of information outweighs the ability to navigate it.

One important trait that can help new librarians and archivists categorize and search through the sheer quantity of information is a love of history. History teaches people to make connections between ages, events, and people. Knowing where to start looking for a newspaper article on the Spanish-American War or a popular song from the disco era can help you or your future patrons link to related information with ease. Archivists also benefit from a love of history. Whether caretaking a collection of artifacts or historical documents, archivists help preserve history for generations to come. Even though librarians and archivists require education in information systems, having a grounding in history can help you understand the cultural treasures you are making available to all.

Find Out More

Academy of Certified Archivists (ACA)
1450 Western Ave., Suite 101
Albany, NY 12203
phone: (518) 694-8471
website: www.certifiedarchivists.org

The ACA is an independent organization that provides certification for professional archivists. Certified archivists are considered experts in all aspects of archive management.

American Library Association (ALA)

50 E. Huron St.
Chicago, IL 60611-2795
phone: (800) 545-2433
website: www.ala.org

The ALA is the world's oldest and largest library association. Its mission is to help develop, promote, and improve libraries and the profession of librarians.

International Federation of Library Associations (IFLA)

PO Box 95312
2509 CH Den Haag
Netherlands
phone: +31 70 3140884
website: www.ifla.org

The IFLA is an international body representing the interests of library and information services and their users worldwide.

National Archives and Records Administration (NARA)

8601 Adelphi Rd.
College Park, MD 20740-6001
phone: (866) 272-6272
website: www.archives.gov

As the nation's official record keeper, the NARA reviews documents and materials created in the United States and permanently preserves those it deems important for legal or historical reasons.

Public Library Association (PLA)

50 E. Huron St.
Chicago, IL 60611
phone: (800) 5450-2433
website: www.ala.org/pla

The goal of the PLA is to provide or advocate for communication, continuing education, and programming for anyone interested in public libraries.

Society of American Archivists
17 N. State St., Suite 1425
Chicago, IL 60602-4061
phone: (312) 606-0722
website: www2.archivists.org

The Society of American Archivists helps archivists achieve professional excellence in the identification, preservation, and use of records that have enduring value.

Archaeologist

What Do Archaeologists Do?

Every human culture in history has left a visible record of its existence. But many of those civilizations and their people are lost to modern times—buried under desert sands, swallowed up by jungles, covered over by earth, or hidden in caves. It is the job of archaeologists to uncover traces of these ancestors by finding and analyzing the artifacts, or human-made objects, they leave behind. These range from eating utensils to weapons, simple homes to complex tombs, roadways to aqueducts, and terraced hillside farms to garbage dumps. Archaeologists examine places and objects like these for clues about the people who made them. Their efforts reveal facts about history and prehistory to make the story of humanity more complete.

Archaeologists are like historians because they study the past. However, historians largely compose history from records left by our human ancestors at times when recorded history was written down. Archaeologists may work on uncovering facts about civilizations that possessed written records, but they typically focus on the

37

lives of ancient people through the artifacts they left behind. They might sift through people's belongings in a search for clues about daily life that might have seemed so ordinary to people at the time that nobody thought to write about them. There have also been people who never learned to write or for whom writing was forbidden or discouraged, such as African American slaves in the United States. By looking at the artifacts they left behind, archaeologists can find clues about these cultures that might be invisible to historians searching only through written records.

To locate and uncover evidence of past civilizations, archaeologists spend time in libraries, on the Internet, and at dig sites where ancient people were known to live, work, trade, worship, fight, and die. For example, Professor Charles Stanish of the University of California–Los Angeles has visited Neolithic dig sites in Peru to reveal how warfare shaped even early civilizations. In a 2012 interview with HistoryNet.com, for example, Stanish notes that movement of early people up the Peruvian hillsides suggests an increasing concern for their own defense:

> The very first settled villages are in river valleys, wide open and in no way defensively postured. Then around a millennium or two BC we see that people start to move up on terraced hills. People are clearly spending a lot of time and effort to be up on top of a hill away from water and away from their fields. People are living on these terraces, which also make very defendable locations. Those are patterns that tell us that people are concerned about raiding. Then from around 300 BC to about AD 700 we begin to see the rise of the great fortresses, massive walled things.

To make such observations, Stanish and other archaeologists spend a lot of time outside, sometimes in inhospitable environments and even underwater. While much information about locations and ancient people can be found in history books, archaeologists generally love to be out in the field working on their hands and knees, meticulously unearthing buried artifacts. Sometimes these artifacts seem to fit in with what is already known about a civilization; sometimes a new find might contradict or add to what is known. For many archaeologists, fitting together the pieces of the historical puzzle or simply discovering buried ancient treasures is what makes the job exciting. In a National *Geographic Kids* interview, Fredrik Hiebert, a former University of Pennsylvania professor and a current curator at the National Gallery of Art, relates the joy of finding artifacts during an Egyptian excavation along the Red Sea:

> We were excavating this [merchant's] house, and we finished the excavation, and there was a reed mat in front of the house that was still preserved. This was about a 700-year-old reed mat. And we were done with our excavations, and I had taken drawings. I had done drawings of the house, and we had photographed it, and I thought "Gee, it's a shame to leave this reed mat here on the ground."
> So I pulled it up, and then we made a really interesting discovery. Underneath the mat was the house key the merchant had left 700 years ago and he had hid his key underneath the door mat, thinking he would return one day. And it even had his name written on it.

The Significance of Luck

"I always get excited finding new things, however mundane they might be. On one of the first digs I went on, when I was still at high school, I found a tower on the Roman wall around Cambridge. I remember being very proud of that—even though I had just been lucky!"

Ian Hodder, quoted in Society for California Archaeology, "Dr. Ian Hodder," 1999. https://scahome.org.

These small discoveries can tell a lot about the people who lived long ago. Their aspirations, their daily tasks, and their habits reveal traits that are not so far removed from people today. Of course, archaeologists sometimes make grand discoveries—such as the uncovering of the intact tomb of King Tutankhamun in 1922, but more often archaeologists make small findings that, when connected to other discoveries, help fill in the story of the past.

Are All Archaeologists Alike?

Human history spans the globe and extends thousands of years into the past. Different cultures have survived during the same time periods but in different places, and different cultures have also lived in the same places but at different times. With so much to study all around the world, archaeologists tend to specialize in studying just one thing—usually a particular culture, time period, and location will grab their interest.

Classical archaeology, for example, is the study of the cultures of the ancient Greeks and Romans and is a popular and well-known specialty of the science. Many people also think of the ancient Egyptians—their pyramid tombs and the golden sarcophagus of King Tutankhamun—when they think of archaeology, and that's a specialty, too. So are the ancient cultures of Asia and South America—the Great Wall of China or the remains of the fifteenth-century Incan fortress of Machu Picchu in the mountains of Peru are definitely of interest to archaeologists.

Some specialties of archaeology are not as obvious. Ethnoarchaeologists study the history and development of ethnic cultures that still exist, such as the Inuit people native to North America. These archaeologists compare evidence from the tools and other things their ancestors made and used with the lifestyle and cultural values these people still have today. Biblical archaeologists seek to unearth and study artifacts that might give factual clues to the stories told in the Bible. Underwater archaeology is concerned with investigating things like shipwrecks or cities that have been covered by water, searching for objects that tell what those people's lives were like. Urban archaeologists study the buildings and layouts of cities, often focusing on a particular metropolis and time period, such as New York City in the 1800s or Maui, Hawaii, up until the 1950s. Archaeology is a wide and varied field, and there is something within it to interest almost anyone.

An archaeologist examines an ancient artifact. Archaeologists study early human societies by finding and analyzing the objects they leave behind.

There's More to Archaeology than Digging in the Dirt

Archaeology has been glorified in movies (most notably those featuring the fictional archaeologist Indiana Jones) as a highly adventurous career of digging in often exotic places and finding priceless treasures. Most archaeologists *do* lead or participate in excavations—projects that involve unearthing buried objects or places—but that is certainly not all they do. In fact, most spend a considerable amount of their time in offices or libraries conducting research on their area of interest. Head of the Oakland, California, archaeology firm Archeo-Tech, Allen G. Pastron states in an October 2010 edition of *Amazing Kids! Magazine*, "Long before we do any digging, we conduct extensive historical research at the library about the site we are planning to excavate and the era when the site was occupied. The more you know about the people, places and important events you wish to study, the better you will be able to understand and interpret the physical remains that are uncovered." In addition, there are usually many regulations and procedures an archaeologist must go through long before any actual digging or excavation can be performed. Local governments and groups of citizens, for example, usually must review the archaeologist's plans and purpose and give permission for the dig.

During an excavation, archaeologists usually need a team of helpers. The work can be daunting. Once artifacts are unearthed, smaller ones must be transported to laboratories, where they are carefully cleaned, sorted, organized, and cataloged. Larger artifacts, such as remnants of buildings, may have to be studied on-site.

Excavations can take months or even years, but archaeologists can expect to spend more time analyzing the things they dig up than actually doing the digging itself. They carefully study their relics and write reports about their findings and conclusions. They are also responsible, in many cases, for preserving the artifacts. They may work with museums or preservation organizations to ensure that rare, old, or unique artifacts are kept safe and intact for future generations of people to study.

Altogether, archaeology is often more of an indoor job than an outdoor one. Archaeologists are both historians and scientists—research and work in the laboratory are a large part of what they do. Many archaeologists also teach at colleges or universities. Most archaeologists, in fact, have busy careers working for museums, colleges or universities, consulting firms, or even the government, and most of that work is done indoors. Before you consider the job of archaeologist, recognize that these professionals are responsible not only for uncovering the past but recording it, writing about it, and presenting it to others.

What It Takes to Be an Archaeologist

Professional archaeologists are scholars, first and foremost. The minimum requirement for finding work in this field, such as at a museum, a college or university, or in a government agency, is a graduate degree in archaeology (or in anthropology, which is the study of human culture and is closely related to archaeology). A master's degree or a doctorate is not the only credential archaeologists might need, however. Equally important is experience doing the actual work of an archaeologist—things like participating in excavations, cataloging findings, and preserving historic artifacts. Aspiring archaeologists usually obtain this hands-on experience during their college course work—they might have a professor who is organizing an excavation, for example, and they might volunteer to spend a summer assisting on the dig. This can be hard work. It also may require sleeping in tents alongside the dig, and it usually comes with little or no pay. However, it is one way to gain the experience necessary to later find a paying job as an archaeologist.

People who are well suited to this career field tend to be detail oriented, are fascinated by history, and enjoy research. A sense of adventure, the desire to travel, and the ability to learn about and feel comfortable with different cultures also helps suit somebody to a career as an archaeologist. Physical fitness, too, is important if an aspiring archaeologist intends to organize or participate in excavations, because they often require long days of hard physical work—with few to no vacation days or even weekends, in many cases—until the dig is complete.

As with other history-related careers, archaeology requires strong writing skills, since an archaeologist typically writes about his or her findings in books, scientific journals, and other resources.

Putting the Pieces Together

"To be successful as a professional archaeologist, a wide array of diverse skills is required. First, and perhaps most important, you must have an active imagination and the ability to see possibilities that may not be readily apparent. This is because an archaeologist is required to take scattered bits and pieces of sometimes seemingly unrelated data and try to recreate the ways in which groups of people lived long ago."

Allen G. Pastron, quoted in Sean Traynor, "Interview with Dr. Allen G. Pastron, Archaeologist," *Amazing Kids! Magazine*, October 2010. http://mag.amazing-kids.org.

Knowledge of foreign languages—both modern and ancient, such as Latin or ancient Greek—can also help an archaeologist be a successful scholar of the cultures he or she is especially interested in researching.

Archaeologists tend to gravitate toward this profession out of a passion for the subject matter, not necessarily for the money. According to the Bureau of Labor Statistics (BLS), a typical archaeologist can expect to earn an average of about $59,000 a year, but archaeologists may make as little as $45,000 to more than $100,000 yearly. Archaeologists who are considered experts in their field often earn higher wages by supplementing their income with activities like consulting, teaching, or speaking at conferences or meetings.

Finding a job as an archaeologist may require some flexibility, too. Although the BLS indicates that this field is growing faster than the average occupation, there are not many openings for archaeologists, and competition for them may be strong. In an interview with the website for the Society for California Archaeology, University of California–Santa Barbara professor Brian Fagan warns, "There are not enough jobs, and certainly few top ones. Do you have the fire in your belly and the PASSION, which makes for a lifelong love of the subject? If not, don't touch it." People who are interested in archaeology can increase their chances of finding a job by seeking and participating in current archaeology digs or projects or taking a temporary position analyzing artifacts in a laboratory. Such positions are a way for beginning archaeologists to gain work experience and make money, and they may lead to a steady, full-time career.

Find Out More

Archaeological Institute of America (AIA)
Boston University
656 Beacon St., 6th Floor
Boston, MA 02215-2006
phone: (617) 353-9361
website: www.archaeological.org

The AIA's goals include promoting an understanding of the material record of humanity's past and fostering an appreciation of diverse cultures. It supports archaeologists, their research, and the preservation of the world's archaeological resources.

Institute of Nautical Archaeology (INA)
PO Drawer HG
College Station, TX 77841-5137
phone: (979) 845-6694
website: http://nauticalarch.org

The INA is a nonprofit international research organization that focuses on archaeological sites of nautical significance, such as shipwrecks and submerged ruins.

Register of Professional Archaeologists
3601 E. Joppa Rd.
Baltimore, MD 21234
phone: (410) 931-8100
website: http://Rpanet.org

The Register of Professional Archaeologists maintains a listing of archaeologists who have agreed to abide by an explicit code of conduct and standards of research performance. It has developed and enforces a set of professional standards in archaeology.

Society for American Archaeology (SAA)
1111 Fourteenth St. NW, Suite 800
Washington, DC 20005-5622
phone: (202) 789-8200
website: www.saa.org

The SAA provides a variety of resources to support archaeologists and encourage them to undertake public education and outreach.

Society for Commercial Archeology (SCA)
PO Box 2500
Little Rock, AR 72203
website: http://sca-roadside.org

The SCA is a national organization devoted to the buildings, artifacts, structures, signs, and symbols of the twentieth-century commercial landscape. It offers publications, conferences, and tours to help preserve and celebrate structures and archaeology.

Intelligence Analyst

What Is Intelligence Analysis?

Since the terrorist attacks against the United States on September 11, 2001, the need for trained intelligence professionals in America has risen. The FBI alone states that its number of intelligence analysts has tripled in the years following that tragedy. The FBI, though, is not alone in utilizing intelligence analysts. The CIA, the National Security Agency (NSA), and the military all require the skills of analysts to make sense of the reports of field agents who gather information on possible foreign and domestic threats or other matters that might impact American diplomatic, trade, or military policy. Even some private companies that contract with the government hire intelligence analysts. If you are interested in figuring out codes or difficult problems, examining other cultures and their histories, or putting together disparate pieces of information to create a snapshot of an event, person, country, or pressing issue, you might have what it takes to be an intelligence analyst.

Intelligence analysts work with others in the profession to piece together bits of information to create a better

Understanding the World

"I think the intelligence analyst's mission is less about 'connecting the dots' (although sometimes it is) or predicting the future (although sometimes it is) or speaking truth to power (although we often do) than it is about understanding the world. . . . An understanding of history and culture is key. . . . And I am not talking about our history and culture, but the history and culture of the countries we work on *as the people and leaders of those countries understand them.*"

Martin Petersen, "What I Learned in 40 Years of Doing Intelligence Analysis for US Foreign Policymakers," *Studies in Intelligence*, March 2011. www.cia.gov.

understanding of a subject. The information may come from field agents or be gleaned from news services, foreign contacts, books and magazines, satellite images, and any other relevant sources. Typically, these bits of information are used to help the government or military decide the best course of action to take in response to events such as a developing water crisis in a foreign land, a pattern of domestic terrorism, or the flow of refugees across borders following a civil war. Many times, this information is shared with other nations involved in a matter of international or global importance; sometimes the information is kept secret because it may jeopardize national security.

Not all intelligence analysts do the same tasks. Some work with maps, some work with encrypted codes, some collect data from agents, and some do a variety of other work. In the FBI, for example, tactical analysts tend to be closely connected to their sources and field agents, providing assistance to these individuals in a timely manner. Sally Rall, an FBI intelligence analyst, states on the FBI website, "If an agent needs to get in the car and go arrest someone before that person hurts somebody, the agent can call [a tactical intelligence analyst] for vital information—information that can save lives." Strategic intelligence analysts, on the other hand, deal with larger issues and connections. Thus, while a tactical analyst might be concerned with organizing field agents who are gathering information on oil-drilling practices in Saudi Arabia, a strategic analyst might be focused on how drilling and the movement of oil impacts the Middle East and its relationship to other global regions. If you like computers, the NSA as well as the CIA and FBI employ cyberintelligence analysts. They trace messages and broadcasts from various groups and countries in an attempt to locate threats or hazards to US interests. What data is analyzed and how it is analyzed is as varied as the myriad ways information is transferred in the modern age. Of course, analysts commonly must be able to amass information from numerous types of sources, but choosing a specialty can help you work with the tools that most interest you.

On the Job: Organizing and Analyzing

You might think from their connection to the world of spying that intelligence analysts live a romantic life filled with danger and adventure. However, analysts are not field agents; their primary concern is organizing data and figuring out how the bits and pieces can be put together to inform policy or military decisions. (In 2015 alone, the FBI's Computer Analysis Response Team examined 37,600 pieces of media totaling more than 9.77 petabytes, or 9,770 terabytes, of data while supporting more than 7,338 investigations.) Most work in offices each day, using a computer to help organize their work and communicate with others. They may work long hours and weekends, depending on the project at hand. They coordinate their knowledge with other analysts and draft papers on the topics they are studying. Analysts commonly report their findings to a section or bureau chief, who brings the information to executives or military strategists in Washington, DC.

Analysts typically work within a specified field that focuses on a specific country (such as China), an international zone (such as southern Africa), or a narrower pursuit within a geographic region (trade relations, for example, or the environment). Intelligence analysts become experts in their specializations, giving informed explanations of subject matter to those who might not understand the details or inner workings of a crucial event. Sometimes analysts must travel to foreign lands or be assigned to an overseas embassy to get a better idea of what is at stake in a region. They might consort with foreign intelligence officers or be called on to speak to concerned officials either at home or abroad. One unnamed intelligence analyst quoted on the CIA website believes the variety of assignments is one of the perks of the job. "I've been able to have a wide range of experiences—from briefing senior U.S. officials to traveling to countries that I never imagined seeing," the analyst states, "and I haven't had to switch employers to do it!"

Most of the information that analysts deal with is highly classified. The work of analysts is monitored to make sure they do not divulge anything that would endanger others or compromise government policy. Intelligence analysts do not commonly talk about their work because of its classified nature. The CIA website even recommends that people interested in becoming analysts not discuss this interest with family or friends.

Education and Training

If you are considering a job in government or military intelligence, you will need relevant education and training. The FBI and CIA career web pages note that intelligence analysts should have a bachelor's or master's degree in fields such as history, political science, geography, international studies, national security, or statistics. Both the FBI and the CIA state that history majors often find work in the intelligence community, likely because they have a broader knowledge of historical events and connections between events. In addition, history majors often possess a talent for research and writing. The FBI and CIA career pages add that for this job, "Excellent analytical and problem-solving skills, well-developed interpersonal skills, excellent briefing skills, and an ability to convey complex information in a clear, concise manner

Interning with the CIA

"We have a very robust internship program for students at both the undergraduate and graduate levels. These are paid internships that students can apply for as early as their sophomore year. Interns in the DI [Directorate of Intelligence] are matched with a mentor to work on real, substantive intelligence issues. We are not just offering these students summer employment, but potentially a career. Therefore, we want them to truly understand the business of analysis and be able to make an informed decision about a career here."

Jami Miscik, quoted in *Black Collegian*, "Interview with Jami Miscik of the CIA," October 1, 2004. www.thefreelibrary.com.

are also required." Many of these traits are shared by history majors as well as other liberal arts students.

Pursuing a foreign language in school can also help in intelligence work, since certain tasks may require reading foreign documents, understanding different cultures, and interacting with people from other countries. Being fluent in or at least familiar with multiple languages will make you a stronger candidate for many intelligence jobs and may outweigh even the importance of a degree. History majors may have a leg up in these skills because they often have taken some courses in foreign languages, and they commonly have some sense of world events and politics from other general classes in their field of study. However, a strong résumé in other aspects of intelligence analysis may be enough to get you in the door, and the study of a foreign language and culture may be undertaken as you develop other skills within an intelligence community.

Both the military and government agencies teach their personnel the skills required to function in a given field of intelligence work. On its website, the FBI states that new analysts undergo a ten-week Intelligence Basic Course at the training facility in Quantico,

Virginia, "where they learn critical thinking skills, research and analysis techniques, and communications skills, as well as how to produce a variety of intelligence reports and briefings." Learning how to compile reports and perform briefings is key to the job because analysts must be able to communicate their findings to others. During such courses, you may also learn complex computer databases or take language classes as part of your assignments.

Various colleges also offer programs specifically in intelligence work to help prospective candidates acquire an edge in landing a job. Courses might focus on the history of intelligence work, communications, cryptology, and politics of specific geographical regions. However, no special training is required beyond a postsecondary education in a field relevant to intelligence work. Candidates are accepted from a variety of college majors, as long as they can demonstrate the traits intelligence agencies are looking for.

Wait, There's More

Other requirements of the position have less to do with training and education. For example, an intelligence analyst must be a US citizen to work for the FBI or CIA. He or she must also undergo a physical exam, psychological exam, polygraph (lie detector) test, and a background check. So keep in mind that having the necessary education may not be enough to land a job with a government agency. In addition, intelligence analysts who work for the military are typically military personnel first and therefore must complete military training. Even the FBI and CIA often consider military service a plus for applying for intelligence work, so you may consider taking this route in building up the experience to apply for the position of intelligence analyst in either military or government agencies.

Landing a Job and Earning a Living

Intelligence agencies stress that competition for intelligence jobs is tough, even as these organizations are expanding their intelligence networks in the age of global terrorism. College students hoping for an opportunity to work in intelligence analysis must have a grade point average of at least a 3.0 on a 4.0 scale. Having foreign language skill or other unique offerings (such as participation in university political organizations or debate teams) can certainly make you stand out from the crowd of other high-performing students hoping to enter the field. "I have met incredibly brilliant people who are analysts here," Rall says of the FBI. "There are lawyers, scientists, people who are multi-lingual, national and international experts in their fields with priceless institutional knowledge going back over 20 years." Standing out from the crowd and fitting in with these experts is an important means of landing an intelligence job.

If you do get hired, you should not expect that your training or education will end. Intelligence analysts are continually being taught new skills and often attend classes in changing political situations, foreign languages, or new technologies. On its website, the CIA states that "agency analysts are encouraged to maintain and broaden professional ties through academic study, contacts, and attendance at professional meetings." Keeping up with a changing world is part of the excitement of the position.

According to the online salary information company PayScale, intelligence analysts make a median salary of $69,000. Those who work in the private sector (as government contractors) may receive bonuses and profit-sharing opportunities that significantly boost their pay. In addition, experience level can affect pay. The CIA, for example, gives a salary range of roughly $51,000 to $99,000, which is tied to experience. Government employees (and most contractors) receive other benefits such as health care as well as base salary. Intelligence analysts are also called upon to travel the world as part of their professional duties. In this way interacting with different cultures and meeting new people are perks of the job. Sometimes analysts may vie for new assignments in foreign lands, thus giving them opportunities to live in various parts of the globe that they otherwise would not see.

Although intelligence analysts may not engage in the highly fictionalized exploits of James Bond, they help their agencies through the application of their knowledge. They are able to see things that others might miss, and they can make connections between people, places, and events that can help keep the nation safe. If you are interested in history and international relations, intelligence analysis can be a rewarding field.

Find Out More

Central Intelligence Agency (CIA)
Office of Public Affairs
Washington, DC 20505
phone: (703) 482-0623
website: www.cia.gov

The CIA is a government agency that gathers and analyzes intelligence from overseas. Though not a law enforcement agency, the CIA gathers information that may be shared with law enforcement partners around the world. The agency's website provides career information on those seeking positions in its intelligence network.

Department of Homeland Security (DHS)
Office of Intelligence and Analysis
phone: (202) 282-8000
website: www.dhs.gov

Organized in the wake of the 2001 terrorist attacks on the United States, the DHS is a government agency that monitors and gathers intelligence on domestic and foreign threats to the nation. Its Office of Intelligence and Analysis uses intelligence analysts to assess threats and provide information that can be used to coordinate proper responses to those threats.

Federal Bureau of Investigation (FBI)
935 Pennsylvania Ave. NW
Washington, DC 20535-0001
phone: (202) 324-3000
website: www.fbi.gov

The FBI is the nation's chief law enforcement agency concerned with intelligence and national security. It functions as part of the US Department of Justice and has numerous field offices throughout the United States. Anyone interested in intelligence jobs with the FBI can consult its website to find the relevant job description and requirements.

National Security Agency (NSA)
9800 Savage Rd.
Fort Meade, MD 20755
phone: (301) 688-6524
website: www.nsa.gov

The NSA is a US government agency, under the US Department of Defense, tasked with electronic surveillance and monitoring of global communications networks. It is also charged with protecting US communications networks from attack or espionage. The NSA employs many intelligence analysts who often specialize in cybersystems monitoring.

Museum Curator

What Kinds of Museums Are There?

Museums come in all shapes and sizes. You may have visited a local county museum that fills a two-story house in your community, or perhaps you have entered one of the nineteen buildings that make up the Smithsonian Institution in Washington, DC. Regardless of what these structures look like, all museums share an interest in preserving and exhibiting collections of things to the public. America's Car Museum in Tacoma, Washington, is a huge hangar-shaped building that holds the world's largest private car collection, with more than five hundred vehicles. The State Tretyakov Gallery in Moscow houses more than 130,000 Russian art exhibits, including fifteenth-century painter Andrei Rublev's *Trinity*, a famed religious icon depicting the Christian Holy Trinity. And about a half-million visitors stop each year at Leeds Castle in Kent, England, to see the 130 pieces displayed in its Dog Collar Museum. Everything from sports achievements, to aircraft history, to human hair has been the focus of museum collections. The mission of museums is to collect and display these items. A museum curator's job is to help in this mission.

What Does a Museum Curator Do?

A museum curator is a person who knows enough about the subject matter or topic area of the museum to know what kinds of items should have a place in it. The curator makes decisions about what to include in a museum and may also have a role in finding interesting objects that fit the museum's goals. Curators also keep records of the items in the museum and oversee the maintenance and preservation of these objects. A curator is usually among the most highly educated of a museum's employees, but can still be amazed and puzzled by a unique object and want to find out more about it. Ellen Taubman of the Museum of Arts and Design in New York City is the curator of an exhibit of Native American arts. She recalls, "Looking at amazing pieces of beadwork, I would think, what was this woman doing, what was she trying to do with the patterns? You knew there was some personalization, but you never knew what it was." Often these curiosities lead curators to develop exhibits that seek to answer such questions, making fascinating displays that will charm and educate the public as well.

Once a museum has amassed a collection of objects, it needs to put them on display for visitors. Curators may work with exhibit designers, people who specialize in making interesting exhibits, to bring exhibits to life. Objects might be hung on walls, arranged in display cases, or propped in scenic settings. If items are particularly fragile, unique, or valuable, they must be arranged where visitors cannot touch them. Some exhibits may need special security measures to protect against theft. Other components of a museum might include walking paths through the museum, background music, sound effects, and lighting. The exhibit designer's job is to care for objects but also to show them off in an interesting and memorable way.

Curators also commonly work with education specialists— people who help teach the public about the exhibits on display. Every collection, or even each individual item, typically needs a label, a plaque, or some other written description telling visitors what it is and why it's interesting. Such information is sometimes interactive—visitors might push a button to see a simulation of something or hear a recorded explanation, for example. Many museums offer walking tours, during which visitors can take headphones and listen to explanations at different exhibits. Other museums include exhibits that allow visitors to touch, move, or play with things. Education specialists usually do a lot of research to make sure that every object displayed in the museum is explained correctly but also in an interesting and memorable way. They may also help market or publicize what the museum has to offer.

Depending on the size of the museum, curators may function in some of these roles. For example, a small museum might require that its curatorial staff also design the exhibits and provide the educational information for each display. A larger museum might employ numerous people to fill these roles individually. Thus, if you are interested in working for a museum, find out what the responsibilities of each post entail. With experience in history, you may be attracted to only the job of curating collections, or if you have some design talent, you might find that this skill combined with a love of history would lead you to prefer designing exhibit spaces for the public. Also, working in a large museum that has different types of exhibits may allow you to work with a particular specialty or interest of yours so that you can bring much more enthusiasm to the job.

A Curator's Workday

If you work in a museum, you could be called on to do a number of tasks on any given day. Small museums may have few employees, and therefore everyone might have multiple tasks. Once a museum is established, making decisions about which objects to add to a museum's collection might be only a small part of the job, even for a curator. Much of the work done in a museum might instead involve caring for the objects the museum does display. Other daily tasks might include reviewing and updating educational materials, negotiating the loan of artworks from other museums, conducting marketing activities that inform the public about the museum and what it offers, fund-raising, and venturing into the community to give presentations about the museum or its exhibits at schools and special events.

Once a museum's standard exhibits have been put on display, they may not change much or often. Many museums, however, host temporary, traveling museum exhibits, and these can give extra variety to the collection. Traveling exhibits move from one museum to another, and curators might travel with these exhibits to give presentations about the materials on display or be on hand to help answer questions. A job with a traveling museum exhibit might be an adventurous alternative to working for a traditional museum if you want to visit and work in many different cities.

Beyond these tasks associated with the collections, a curator is also expected to spend a lot of time doing original research that can help expand the knowledge about the items within a collection. Ashlee Whitaker, curator of religious art at the Brigham Young University Museum of Art, remarks in an October 2015 interview on the museum's website, "A curator will come up with a [display] concept, and then explore the concept by doing a lot of research." To find the appropriate pieces for her exhibits, she explains,

> I have spent months hunting for the right works of art to convey a certain idea or that exemplifies an artist. I use a lot of different online art and museum databases. I look

through other museums' collections if they are online and if not, I may just contact their museum and speak with curators or collections managers to see if they have relevant artworks. Also, I've also found works of art through books and word of mouth. Things start coming out of the woodwork and it's so exciting!

In addition to researching, curators do a lot of writing, presenting the findings of their research as well as doing book reviews or other critical pieces within their field of interest.

Preparing for a Museum Curator Job

A museum curator typically needs a master's degree or, preferably, a doctorate in the museum's area of interest. Another option is to pursue a degree in museum studies and a second degree in an area or topic of specialization, such as history, zoology, or a particular culture—it all depends on the kind of museum where you think you might like to work. Small museums may employ curators with less educational experience. Large museums usually look for individuals who have PhDs and have made contributions to the field—in terms of academic writing and publishing—because the museum expects the curator will continue to make contributions.

If you aren't sure you want to pursue a higher degree, that doesn't mean you can't work in a museum. Larger museums have a need for employees to help set up and maintain exhibits, work at ticket counters or welcome desks, and do many other things. Such entry-level positions could possibly lead to a job with greater responsibility. If museums seem interesting but you aren't sure yet if this would be a good career for you, consider volunteering as a docent (tour guide) or completing an internship at a museum. In a January 2016 interview on the Winchester University History Student's blog, Danielle Sellers, deputy curator at the Royal Engineers Museum in Gillingham, England, states that her attraction to the job of museum curator was gradual. "I had a love of Museums and Galleries from an early age and eventually realised that I wanted to immerse myself in this world," she says. "Initially I had no clear idea of what area I wanted to focus on but volunteering allowed me to work in a few different areas." If you like the work, such positions could help you get a paying job. If you wish to move up to curatorial work, begin studies in the field that interests you or consider museum studies to acquire the necessary advanced degree.

Special Skills and Talents

Curiosity about many different topics is essential for anyone who wants to work in a museum setting. Being detail oriented and a thorough researcher are also important. It helps to be organized, since you might be asked to classify and catalog the different items the museum holds.

Research skills are very important to curators because much of the work will be done independently—reading up on topics, combing the Internet for information, and distilling the significant details. Strong writing skills are also crucial in museum jobs. Not only might you be expected to write materials to explain the museum's exhibits, but you may have to write articles for newspapers, marketing materials sent out to the public, letters to possible financial supporters, and applications for grants to help fund the museum.

Being a good verbal communicator is also important if you want to work in a museum. You may be asked to lead special tours for visitors as well as to make presentations at conferences and other large events, speak to students at schools, or visit professional boards or organizations to speak on behalf of the museum and ask for their support. Museums exist to educate the public, and you will need strong public speaking skills to hold most positions in a museum.

In a January 2014 interview with the University of Michigan Museum of Art website, Rudolf Frieling, curator of media arts at the San Francisco Museum of Modern Art, says he loves his job because "it lets you work with a lot of different people. You're a producer, a diplomat, an essayist, a scholar (maybe), a visionary

Understanding the Past Through Artifacts

"When you think about beadwork or other works, they were all made for a purpose. When I think about the North West Coast, the great masks and bowls, all cultures make things for a purpose. The way these things were embellished were so beautiful, I wish they could speak. The artists themselves can't speak but the works still exist. They are still speaking, just not telling us what we want to know. This gains my respect and admiration. When I see a great piece of Native art, historic or contemporary, I still get weak at the knees."

Ellen Taubman, quoted in *Métis Ramblings* (blog), "Interview with Curator Ellen Taubman, Changing Hands: Art Without Reservation 3, Museum of Arts and Design, New York City," September 9, 2012. http://metisramblings.blogspot.com.

(maybe), a politician (for sure)." While curators wear many hats, as Frieling describes, they typically enjoy bringing the fruits of their labors to the public. Creating interesting and successful exhibits is the joy of curating. According to Frieling, aspiring curators will feel the need to fill "spaces" in the world. He tells future curators, "Do something, write, curate, organize, take the initiative wherever and whenever you can. Imagine an empty space and the world that could happen in that space. If you're good at it, you'll want to do more and you'll make yourself a name step by step."

If you land a job as a curator in the United States, you can expect an average salary of just over $56,000. Job growth is slow and often depends on the retirement of older curators. However, as new collections materialize—especially within the realm of the Internet—new positions may open up. Digital curators are bringing the occupation into the twenty-first century. Archives of digital photos, for example, require curators just as brick-and-mortar museums do. Of course, these curators may not have the varied responsibilities of more traditional curators. Still, some universities grant certificates in digital curation, suggesting how prominent and important this role will be in coming times.

Find Out More

American Alliance of Museums

2451 Crystal Dr., Suite 1005
Arlington, VA 22202
phone: (202) 289-1818
website: www.aam-us.org

The American Alliance of Museums supports thirty thousand museums and their employees by helping with career development, sharing best practices, and advocating for museums of all kinds.

Association of Academic Museums and Galleries

website: http://aamg-us.org

The Association of Academic Museums and Galleries supports educational activities and professional development for academic museums, galleries, and collections.

Association of Science and Technology Centers (ASTC)

818 Connecticut Ave. NW, 7th Floor
Washington, DC 20006-2734
phone: (202) 783-7200
website: www.astc.org

The ASTC is an organization of science centers and museums that seeks to establish and enhance relationships between these centers and the public.

International Council of Museums (ICOM)

General Secretariat
Maison de l'UNESCO
1 rue Miollis
75732 Paris Cedex 15
France
phone: +33 (0) 1 47 34 05 00
website: http://icom.museum

The ICOM is a network of more than thirty-five thousand members and museum professionals who represent museums around the world and help respond to the challenges faced by museums.

Western Museums Association (WMA)
PO Box 7042
Tacoma, WA 98417
phone: (707) 433-4701
website: www.westmuse.org

The WMA serves museums and related organizations of the western United States, Canada, and the Pacific Islands, providing vision, enrichment, intellectual challenge, and a forum for communication and interaction.

Lawyer and Paralegal

What Does History Have to Do with a Legal Career?

If you're interested in history, you probably like reading about events that have happened, analyzing them, and creating arguments that they were either the right or the wrong thing to do. As it happens, people in the legal profession do the very same kinds of things—they read, analyze, write, and argue. They have to be good at drawing conclusions from a group of facts and convincing other people that their conclusions make sense. A background in history provides a good foundation for a legal career.

Any legal professional should have at least some knowledge of major events that have shaped the history of the nation, as well as social controversies (think of all the ways civil rights have affected and changed laws), criminal issues (consider battles over alcohol, drugs, and guns), business practices (the history of labor unions come to mind), and other major topics that have created legal stirs over the years. This background is necessary for making strong legal arguments in a court case. It's also important to know legal precedents—similar cases that have come before, what arguments were made in them, and how they turned out. These are the kinds of facts a history buff would enjoy digging up, and it's one of the reasons many history enthusiasts find their way to a legal career.

What Kind of Law Careers Are Out There?

TV shows, movies, and even real-life coverage of major court cases typically portray the legal profession as two lawyers engaged in a battle of wits before a jury and a judge. Usually, the lawyers are fighting over the guilt of a person accused of some violent crime. Criminal cases are certainly a major part of the legal profession, but there is much more to the field of law than what you see on TV or read about in the news, and there are many different career paths you could pursue.

Criminal trials are probably the first thing that comes to mind when you think of the legal profession. Prosecutors are attorneys who work for the government at the local, state, or federal level. They represent the interests of the public and argue that particular people, businesses, or groups are guilty of breaking a law. Defense attorneys serve the interests of their clients in court and attempt to prove either that they are innocent or that they should not be punished for what they were accused of doing. (Some defense attorneys are paid by the government, because the US legal system requires the government to provide a defense lawyer to any accused person who can't afford to or chooses not to pay for one.)

Not all lawyers are involved in criminal practice, however. Many specialize in civil matters concerning complaints of individual people. These are typically lawsuits, in which one party accuses the other of wrongdoing and seeks money in order to make it right. Such cases may include divorce proceedings, personal injury, contract disputes, or product liability. Other lawyers serve mostly as legal advisers, working for companies, organizations, or governmental bodies to help them adhere to laws that may be very complex and changeable.

A lawyer questions a police officer during a court proceeding. Not all lawyers and paralegals spend time in court, but no matter what their specialty they need to be critical thinkers and skilled at analysis and persuasion.

Not all legal professionals are lawyers, either. Judges (who are either elected or appointed to their positions) often have the responsibility of deciding guilt or innocence in court cases or of deciding a fair punishment for people who have been convicted of wrongdoing. Such punishments can include paying fines, serving time in prison, or even being put to death. Judges have a great deal of responsibility, and their decisions become written documents that themselves will be studied by future historians.

Another job within the legal profession is that of paralegal or legal assistant. These people are not actually lawyers, but they work directly for them, assisting with a variety of important legal tasks. Paralegals are persons educated in the law, and they often do research to help lawyers with specific court cases. Among their many duties, they may review legal cases, help the lawyer find and interview witnesses to use in court, verify facts, write drafts of legal documents, and assist in the courtroom. In an interview with CareerColleges.com, Linda McGrath-Cruz, a veteran paralegal of fifteen years, explains some of the traits needed for this job: "Attention to detail is very important, as is having good grammar and communication skills. Being comfortable with technology is a definite plus as many law firms utilize different hardware and software programs, and paralegals need to be able to adapt their tech skills quickly."

How Do I Prepare for a Legal Career?

The type of preparation you need for a law career depends on the kind of job you want. If your goal is to be an attorney, you will first need a bachelor's degree. This can be in any subject, but a history degree can be very useful because it requires students to do a lot of research, writing, and arguing—skills an attorney needs. The next step is to pass the Law School Admission Test (LSAT) and attend law school for the graduate degree required to become a lawyer. Be aware that law schools are notoriously tough to complete; many students fail out of law courses or drop out because of the intense competition and demanding course work. The LawInfo website cautions, "First things first, prepare yourself for a lot of work, the workload is tremendous, but 'workable.' The first year dropout rate, nationwide, hovers around 20 to 40 percent. This sounds high, but it is largely due to the amount of work required to make it through your first year." The three-year program requires students to read, study, and participate in their classes to stay up with the course work. "Some of the professors were ruthless, and some of the students too," recalls one lawyer in a 2013 interview on the Career Action Now career planning website. "They were all brilliant. I felt like an idiot, but I suppose most of my classmates did too. In the end, it taught me to think analytically, support my opinions, and deal with adversity, so it's a good thing I stuck it out." Average tuition for "sticking out" the three years is $90,000, so you must also accept the debt incurred during the program.

Law Is Often a Desk Job

"The biggest surprise new attorneys have is how physically tiring it is to work. This may come as a surprise, but sitting at a desk working all day, often ten hours or more a day, will wear you out until you get accustomed to it. . . . I don't know many young attorneys who didn't think that they were getting mono after their first few months of work. You get used to it, but it takes a while."

Dennis Kennedy, "Twenty Lessons for Lawyers Starting Their Careers," *Law Practice Today*, October 2015. http://apps.americanbar.org.

Following the completion of a law degree, you will need to pass a bar exam, a complex test about all aspects of law and the legal profession. Each state has its own bar exam, and passing it is a requirement for anyone to be licensed to practice law in that state. Once you have a license, you can apply for most any lawyer job in your state. Most aspiring lawyers will seek a job with a firm that works within their specialty, so you should be prepared to specialize in patent law, criminal law, business law, or whatever other field interests you.

Other positions in the law field require less education and preparation. To become a paralegal, for example, you might only need to complete an associate's degree (typically a two-year degree) or a certificate program in paralegal studies. Completing an internship with a law practice can also help aspiring paralegals, giving them both work experience and professional connections that can help them when they start seeking a job.

What Is It like to Work in the Legal Profession?

The lives of legal professionals are often dramatized on television as being full of excitement. Some court cases are, indeed, dramatic in real life. Murder cases often create a big stir in the media, for instance, and the lawyers who argue such cases may gain fame. However, not every legal case has to do with a major crime or is exciting and dramatic. In fact, the vast majority of court cases deal with far less serious issues, ranging from minor crimes like driving offenses or vandalism to civil spats like neighborhood disputes or domestic issues like divorces. Many disputes are settled outside of the courtroom altogether, often with the assistance of lawyers. Some lawyers, such as those who work for businesses, may mostly or entirely provide legal advice to their clients and rarely step into a courtroom at all. On the Blueprint LSAT blog site, Joan Cotkin, a Los Angeles business lawyer, states in a 2010 interview that her days differ if they involve courtroom appearances. She explains, "I usually come into the office between 5:30 am and 6:30 am and put in between 10–12 hours depending on the pending matters. If I am in trial then the work day is intense—usually 16 to 20 hours a day with early am in the office for pretrial prep, late afternoon and evening post trial day review and next day prep and weekend work. Unless I am in trial, I do take weekends off."

Lawyers Are Rarely Bored

"What I love most about being a lawyer is that it never has to be boring. As a lawyer, you always have the opportunity to redesign your practice to accomplish different goals. In 30 years of practice I have seen the way in which law is practiced change radically and rapidly. I hope it keeps on changing."

Howard Finkelstein, quoted in *ABA Journal*, "Why I Love Being a Lawyer," February 2011. www.abajournal.com.

What television often leaves out in its portrayals of lawyers are the less glamorous aspects of the profession. Not only do lawyers argue before a jury, for example, they research laws and similar court cases and write arguments based on this research. Lawyers and paralegals both do a lot of this work, which could actually fill the majority of a typical day. Legal professionals may also spend a lot of time in meetings with their clients or with the lawyers representing the people opposing their clients. Legal professionals in different fields will of course have different types of duties, but engaging in major, high-profile court cases like the ones seen on TV are rarely the norm. In fact, Cotkin reminds prospective lawyers that housekeeping tasks are part of every lawyer's workday. She says that "time sheets, collecting accounts receivable and other aspects of the business of law" are her least favorite activities, even though they are essential to keep her practice going.

Nevertheless, if you are seeking a career in the legal profession, you should be comfortable speaking and arguing in public, whether in meetings and conferences or in the courtroom, as every day in this profession could bring new challenges. Strong persuasive-speaking skills are vital for anyone who wants to be a lawyer. Making compelling oral arguments, whether in courtrooms or boardrooms, is part of most days on the job in the legal profession. A degree in history can prepare you to argue a position based on research and a clear understanding of facts.

Money and Finding Jobs

Lawyers tend to make a decent living. According to the Bureau of Labor Statistics (BLS), attorneys make an average of $115,000 to $175,000 per year. Corporate (business) lawyers who have major companies or organizations as their clients might make substantially more, whereas lawyers who build their practices defending individuals accused of committing crimes might make a lot less because their clients may not be able to afford high fees. (It's also worth noting that most lawyers work much more than forty hours a week to earn their salary.) Prosecuting attorneys who work for the government have a set income that is based on local, state, or federal laws. Judges, too, have a set income but may make anywhere from about $50,000 a year (usually for a local judge) to $175,000 a year (typically a higher-ranking state or federal judge), according to the BLS. Paralegals, by BLS estimates, can typically expect to earn an average of about $47,000 a year.

The legal field is large and varied, so there are many places and ways to find employment in law. Positions as prosecutors or judges are limited, and there is usually a lot of competition for them. But there are many opportunities to find employment with private law firms, to work directly for a company or organization, or to start your own legal practice. Individual people, companies, and organizations often need good legal advice or representation and are willing to pay for it, so hardworking, competent legal professionals can usually find a job, especially if they are willing to consider different kinds of legal practice.

Find Out More

American Bar Association
1050 Connecticut Ave. NW, Suite 400
Washington, DC 20036
phone: (202) 662-1000
website: www.americanbar.org

The American Bar Association promotes excellence in education, competence, ethics, and professionalism for all of the nation's lawyers.

American Civil Liberties Union (ACLU)
125 Broad St., 18th Floor
New York, NY 10004
phone: (212) 549-2500
website: www.aclu.org

The ACLU works to defend individual rights and liberties for all people as guaranteed by the Constitution and laws of the United States. It provides legal information to individuals and groups and resources to anyone interested in law.

American Law Institute
4025 Chestnut St.
Philadelphia, PA 19104
phone: (215) 243-1600
website: www.ali.org

The American Law Institute works to clarify and explain laws that influence courts and legislatures and also helps shape and improve legal education.

National Association of Criminal Defense Lawyers (NACDL)
1660 L St. NW, 12th Floor
Washington, DC 20036
phone: (202) 872-8600
website: www.nacdl.org

The NACDL promotes fairness and due process in criminal justice policy for all people, as well as fair treatment of witnesses and just punishment for the guilty.

National Association of Legal Assistants (NALA)
7666 E. Sixty-First St., #315
Tulsa, OK 74133
phone: (918) 587-6828
website: www.nala.org

NALA provides information and resources about education and certification programs for legal assistants and paralegals, continuing education opportunities for people currently employed in this field, and other resources and support.

National District Attorneys Association (NDAA)
99 Canal Center Pl., Suite 330
Alexandria, VA 22314
phone: (703) 549-9222
website: www.ndaa.org

The goal of the NDAA is to support and provide resources to attorneys who work to protect the rights and safety of American citizens.

INTERVIEW WITH AN ARCHIVIST

Cynthia Laframboise is the state archives manager at the Nevada State Library, Archives and Public Records in Carson City, Nevada. She answered questions about her career by e-mail.

Q: How did you become interested in being an archivist?

A: I became interested in becoming an archivist during my senior year in college. I attended a small Catholic college in Salina, Kansas, and my advisor, Sister Jean McKenna, knew the staff at the Kansas State Historical Society [KSHS] in Topeka. The Historical Society offered three-week internships, and I enrolled in the program. I had one-week projects in the archives, photographs, and manuscript sections. I really enjoyed the internship.

After I graduated from college, I attended the University of Kansas and enrolled in graduate school in history. I earned a Master of Arts degree in history and enrolled in the Historical Administration and Museum Studies program at the University of Kansas. While I was still in the program, I was hired as a library assistant at the Historical Society. I was promoted to archivist a year later. I earned my second Master of Arts degree while I worked full time at the Historical Society. I was then promoted to the State Records Manager at the KSHS. I worked there for 19 years.

Q: Can you describe your typical workday?

A: A typical work day consists of checking e-mail first thing in the morning. If I have a reference request or assignment from the State Archivist, I work on that. I also supervise the Imaging and Preservation Services [IPS] lab, so I go check on projects there. I work with state agencies, local government, and municipalities on different scanning, microfilming, and imaging projects. I usually have paperwork related to IPS. Sometimes it is a statement of work or a local service agreement.

Managing IPS takes up most of my time. Something is always happening in the lab. My archives staff does a great job of handling the reference room and answering requests when we are open to the public. I do some processing of archival collections when I have time.

Q: What do you like most about your job?

A: I work with a talented and dedicated staff, so things run pretty smoothly.

Q: What do you like least?

A: I really get annoyed with our old equipment that breaks down or needs repair. There seem to be constant problems in IPS, whether it is maintaining consistent hot water to process film or the duplicator or processor acting up. It can be frustrating, because when everything works, my staff can crank out work.

Q: What personal qualities do you find most valuable for this type of work?

A: You have to be flexible. Sometimes, whatever you have planned for the day doesn't happen. You need to be able to work independently. Working in state government means that things happened slowly, and I have had to learn to be more patient.

Q: What advice do you have for students who might be interested in this career?

A: You need a history background and an understanding of how government operates. You need to learn the different state agencies and what their functions are in order to better determine which records have historical value. Project management is an important skill to help better manage all the different activities.

Q: What is something about your job that you think would surprise most people?

A: Most people are surprised when I tell them that I am an archivist. Most people have no clue as to what an archivist is. I have to explain what I do.

Q: Can you describe something about your job that was (or is) especially rewarding?

A: I really like it when we are able to find information for people. That is rewarding to me.

Q: What would you say is the biggest challenge you have faced in your job?

A: Trying to juggle two different units—state archives and Imaging and Preservation Services—can be a struggle. We have a very small archives and IPS staff, and sometimes it is hard to keep all the balls in the air.

Q: What was your favorite subject in school, and why?

A: My favorite subject in school was always history. I want to know more about why we are where we are and how we got here. I try to imagine what it would be like to live in a different time, and I am glad that I didn't live back then.

OTHER CAREERS IF YOU LIKE HISTORY

Advertising executive
Anthropologist
Antique dealer
Architect
Auctioneer
Automobile restorer
Business strategist
Chef
Detective
Economist
Editor
Fashion designer
Filmmaker
Financial analyst
Foreign service
Genealogist
Graphic designer

Historic preservationist
Journalist
Lobbyist
Meteorologist
Pawn shop owner
Policy analyst
Political campaign manager
Property appraiser
Public relations specialist
Sommelier (wine expert)
State park manager
Traffic engineer
Translator
Travel agent
Urban planner
Writer

Editor's note: The online *Occupational Outlook Handbook* of the US Department of Labor's Bureau of Labor Statistics is an excellent source of information on jobs in hundreds of career fields, including many of those listed here. The *Occupational Outlook Handbook* may be accessed online at www.bls.gov/ooh.

INDEX